W9-BIA-775

Coins

By Dana Meachen Rau

Reading consultant: Susan Nations, M.Ed., author/literacy coach/consultant

 Gareth Stevens
Publishing

Please visit our Web site www.garethstevens.com. For a free color catalog of all our high-quality books, call toll free 1-800-542-2595 or fax 1-877-542-2596.

Library of Congress Cataloging-in-Publication Data

Rau, Dana Meachen, 1971–
     Coins / by Dana Meachen Rau.
        p. cm. — (Money and banks)
     Includes bibliographical references and index.
     ISBN: 978-1-4339-3377-6 (lib. bdg.)
     ISBN: 978-1-4339-3378-3 (softcover)
     ISBN: 978-1-4339-3379-0 (6-pack)
———1. Coins—United States—Juvenile literature. I. Title. II. Series.
     CJ1830.R38   2005
     332.4'042'0973—dc22   2005042248

New edition published 2010 by
Gareth Stevens Publishing
111 East 14th Street, Suite 349
New York, NY 10003

New text and images this edition copyright © 2010 Gareth Stevens Publishing

Original edition published 2006 by Weekly Reader® Books
An imprint of Gareth Stevens Publishing
Original edition text and images copyright © 2006 Gareth Stevens Publishing

Art direction: Haley Harasymiw, Tammy West
Page layout: Daniel Hosek, Dave Kowalski
Editorial direction: Kerri O'Donnell, Barbara Kiely Miller

Photo credits: Cover, title page, pp. 14, 19 Shutterstock.com; pp. 4, 11, 16 Gregg Andersen; pp. 5 (penny, nickel, dime, quarter, half dollar), 6, 12, 13, 14, 15, 17, 18, 20, 21 Diane Laska-Swanke; p. 5 (golden dollar), 7 courtesy Wikimedia Commons; pp. 8, 9, 10 Dave Kowalski/© Weekly Reader Early Learning Library.

Printed in the United States of America

CPSIA compliance information: Batch #WW10GS: For further information contact Gareth Stevens, New York, New York at 1-800-542-2595.

Table of Contents

Boldface words appear in the glossary.

So Many Coins!

Coins make a clinking sound when you drop them into a piggy bank. Coins are a type of **currency**. Currency is the kind of money people use. In the United States, we use dollars as our currency. One dollar is made up of one hundred cents. Coins are cents.

Some children save their coins in a piggy bank.

Coins are made in six different amounts. A penny is worth one cent. A nickel is worth five cents. A dime is worth ten cents. A quarter is worth twenty-five cents. A half-dollar is worth fifty cents. A golden dollar is worth one dollar. In 2007, the U.S. government began making dollar coins showing the U.S. presidents.

| penny | nickel | dime |
| quarter | half-dollar | golden dollar |

A penny has a brownish color. Nickels, dimes, quarters, and half-dollars look silver. The golden dollar looks gold. Coins are made of mixtures of metals called **alloys**. The alloys used to make coins are copper, zinc, and nickel.

Most U.S. coins are a silver color.

How Coins Are Made

Coins are made by the United States Mint. The word **mint** means to make coins. The United States Mint makes between sixty-five million and eighty million coins every day! Many machines are needed to make coins.

The U.S. Mint makes coins in Denver and Philadelphia (above). You can visit the U.S. Mint to see how coins are made.

First, a flat sheet of metal is fed into a machine called a blanking press. The blanking press works like a cookie cutter. It cuts small, coin-sized circles out of the metal. These circles are called **blanks**. Blanks are the size and shape of coins, but there are no pictures on them.

A blanking press cuts coin-sized circles out of metal sheets.

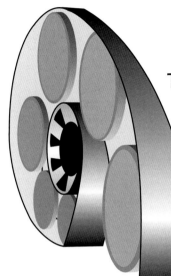

The blanks are heated and cleaned. Then they are put into an upsetting machine. This machine raises the edges of the blanks. The higher edges of the coins keep them from wearing out too quickly.

An upsetting machine puts a raised edge around each blank.

The blanks then go into a machine called a coining press. The coining press stamps a picture on each side of the blank. Then an **inspector** checks each coin to make sure it is perfect. The new coins are counted, then poured into bags. The bags are sent to banks around the country.

A coining press can make 750 coins every minute. That's 45,000 coins an hour!

Coins Up Close

Have you ever flipped a coin to help you make a choice? The front of a coin is called "heads." The back of a coin is called "tails." If the coin lands heads up, you might choose chocolate ice cream. If it lands tails up, you might choose vanilla.

Flipping a coin can help you make a choice.

Abraham Lincoln

Look closely at a coin. The front sides of most coins have **portraits**, or pictures, of U.S. presidents on them. The penny has a portrait of Abraham Lincoln on it. The nickel, dime, quarter, and half-dollar have presidents on them, too. The golden dollar has a portrait of Sacagawea. She was a Native American woman who helped explorers in early America. The new presidential dollar coins each show one U.S. president.

Thomas Jefferson

Franklin D. Roosevelt

George Washington

Sacagawea

John F. Kennedy

The backs of coins have pictures of American **symbols** on them. An eagle is on the back of the half-dollar. The backs of some coins show government buildings. Most pennies have the Lincoln Memorial on them. In 2005, the U.S. Mint made new nickels. Some show an American bison, or buffalo, on the back. Some show a picture of the Pacific Ocean.

Buildings and animals are shown on the backs of some coins.

All coins except the penny and the nickel have grooves along their edges. These grooves are called **reeds**. The reeds help blind people tell different coins apart. The penny and dime are nearly the same size. The dime has reeds, but the penny does not. A blind person would be able to tell the difference between them.

reeds

Each dime has 118 reeds along its edge. Each quarter has 119 reeds.

Each coin shows the date it was made and how much it is worth. All coins also show the word "Liberty," which means freedom. They all say "United States of America" and "In God We Trust." Every coin also has the Latin words "E Pluribus Unum." This means "out of many, one." This shows that the fifty states have joined together to form a single country.

"In God We Trust"

"Liberty"

"United States of America"

"E Pluribus Unum"

Coins are small, but a lot of words fit on them.

Coin Collecting

Do you save your coins in a piggy bank to spend later? Some people collect coins that they never plan to spend. Some coin collectors keep their coins in tiny envelopes. Others use albums or folders to hold the coins they collect.

This boy keeps the coins that he collects in a special folder. The folder has a spot for each coin.

Many people collect coins that are no longer made. They may be worth a lot of money, especially if they are in good condition. Coins with printing errors are often worth a lot of money, too. Some old coins were made of real gold or silver. Many people like to collect coins from other countries. You can learn a lot about a country and its history by looking at its coins.

These coins are from different countries. In what ways are they alike? In what ways are they different?

Some people collect state quarters, too. In 1998, the U.S. Mint started making new quarters. By 2008, there were fifty new quarters, one for each state. The fronts

of all the state quarters still look the same. The backs are all different. They have pictures of something each state is famous for. What does the quarter for your state have on it?

You can learn about U.S. states from their quarters.

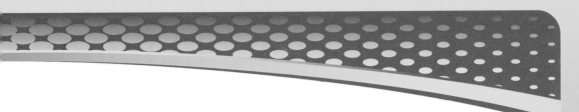

Check the coins in your piggy bank. Do you have the quarter for your state?

If you have the quarter for your state, you may want to save it.

penny = 1 cent   **nickel = 5 cents**   **dime = 10 cents**

Look at the groups of coins below. Think about how much each group is worth. Are the coins on the left more than (>), equal to (=), or less than (<) the coins on the right? The correct answers are on page 23.

1.

2.

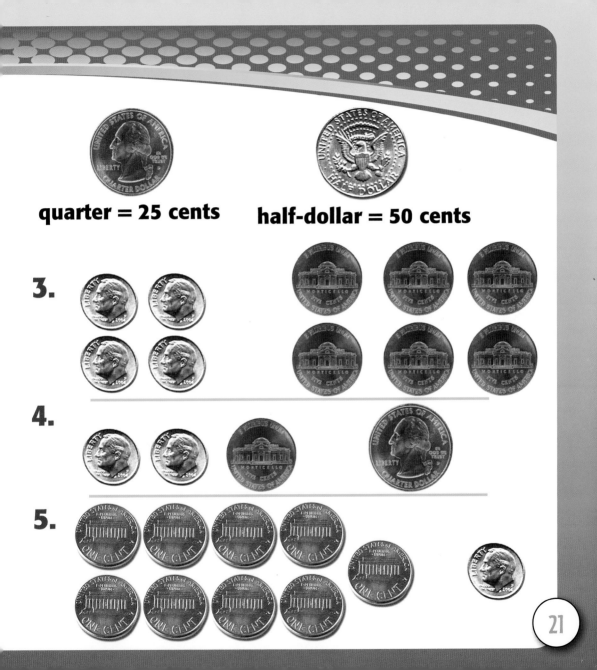

quarter = 25 cents

half-dollar = 50 cents

3.

4.

5.

Glossary

alloys: mixtures of two or more different metals

blanks: circle-shaped pieces of metal that will become coins

currency: the type of money that is used in a country

inspector: a person who checks coins or other things to make sure they have been made correctly

mint: to make coins

portraits: pictures of people's heads and faces

reeds: the grooves along the edges of some coins

symbols: things that stand for or represent other things

For More Information

Books

Hill, Mary. *Pennies*. New York: Children's Press, 2005.

Orr, Tamra. *Coins and Other Currency: A Kid's Guide to Coin Collecting*. Hockessin, DE: Mitchell Lane Publishers, 2009.

Otfinoski, Steve. *Coin Collecting for Kids*. Norwalk, CT: Innovative Kids, 2007.

Web Sites

The Quarter Craze
library.thinkquest.org/CR0212420/main.htm
Learn all about the new quarters and the states they represent

The U.S. Mint for Kids
www.usmint.gov/kids/
Fun facts to learn about and games to play with coins

Publisher's note to educators and parents: Our editors have carefully reviewed these Web sites to ensure that they are suitable for students. Many Web sites change frequently, however, and we cannot guarantee that a site's future contents will continue to meet our high standards of quality and educational value. Be advised that students should be closely supervised whenever they access the Internet.

Math Connection Answer: 1. >   2. <   3. >   4. =   5. <

Index

About the Author

Dana Meachen Rau is an author, editor, and illustrator. She has written more than one hundred books for children, including nonfiction, early readers, and historical fiction. She lives with her family in Burlington, Connecticut.